A BEACON ☉ BIOGRAPHY

ELON MUSK

Tamra B. Orr

PURPLE TOAD
PUBLISHING

PURPLE TOAD
PUBLISHING

Printing   1   2   3   4   5   6   7   8   9

A Beacon Biography

Angelina Jolie
Big Time Rush
Cam Newton
Carly Rae Jepsen
Daisy Ridley
Drake
Ed Sheeran
Ellen DeGeneres
Elon Musk
Harry Styles of One Direction
Jennifer Lawrence
John Boyega
Kevin Durant
Lorde
Malala
Maria von Trapp
Markus "Notch" Persson, Creator of Minecraft
Mo'ne Davis
Muhammad Ali
Neil deGrasse Tyson
Peyton Manning
Robert Griffin III (RG3)

Publisher's Cataloging-in-Publication Data
Orr, Tamra.
  Elon Musk / written by Tamra Orr.
    p. cm.
    Includes bibliographic references, glossary, and index.
ISBN 9781624692567
    1. Musk, Elon—Juvenile literature. 2. Businesspeople—United States—Biography—Juvenile literature. 3. Businesspeople—South Africa—Biography—Juvenile literature. I. Series: Beacon biography.
 HC102.5.M88 2017
 338.762922

Library of Congress Control Number: 2016936316

eBook ISBN: 9781624692574

ABOUT THE AUTHOR: Tamra B. Orr is a full-time author living in the Pacific Northwest. She has written more than 450 educational books for readers of all ages. She is a graduate of Ball State University and commonly gives presentations to schools and conferences. She is fascinated by young people who manage to overcome a rough start and then find a way to make this world a better, safer, and more exciting place to live.

PUBLISHER'S NOTE: This story has not been authorized or endorsed by Elon Musk.

CONTENTS

The launch of Falcon 9 just before Christmas, 2015, was a huge moment in Musk's life.

"Welcome Back, Baby!"

It was now or never.

Billionaire Elon Musk was used to succeeding in everything he did, but if he didn't succeed today, he knew he would be in big trouble. He had launched rockets before, but each one had been a disappointment. The last attempt had been just a few months earlier, in June 2015. Musk and the rest of his SpaceX team were shocked when the rocket exploded just minutes after liftoff. This time, everything had to go right.

The race to be the first company to design, build, and launch a reusable rocket was a hot one. Other billionaires had the same goal, as did huge aerospace companies like Boeing and Lockheed. The demand for carrying cargo into space was growing, but the cost to do so was tremendous. Launches by the National Air and Space Administration (NASA) typically cost $450 million each. Most of the money went to replacing equipment that could be used only once. It burned up in space instead of returning to earth. By creating reusable booster rockets, which Musk and the others were trying to do, each mission would cost only $61 million—a savings of 86 percent.[1]

Amazon founder Jeff Bezos had sent a rocket into space in April 2015. Unfortunately, the propulsion system failed.[2] Virgin Galactic executive Richard Branson launched a rocket a few months later, but it crashed, and one person died. Then, in November 2015, Bezos tried again. This time, his

New Shepard became the first rocket in history to blast off under its own power, soar to the very edge of space, and return to Earth in one piece. It was a great test run—but it was only a test run.

Now, on December 21, 2015, Elon Musk watched his latest rocket, the *Falcon 9*, liftoff without a hitch. This time, instead of bursting into flame, *Falcon 9* soared into space, where it deployed 11 satellites.

Employees from Musk's company screamed with happiness and relief when they saw the stream of the booster lighting up the sky on its way down. As it descended, landing legs came out, allowing the 15-story-tall rocket to land softly right on the landing pad. Musk was thrilled. "Welcome back, baby!" he tweeted.[3]

Designing a rocket like the Falcon 9 will change the way humans explore outer space.

As one SpaceX employee told a local newspaper, the event was "like launching a pencil over the Empire State Building, having it reverse, come back down and land in a shoebox on the ground—in a windstorm."[4]

"It's a revolutionary moment," Musk told reporters about the world's first reusable rocket. "No one has ever brought a booster, an orbital-class booster, back intact."[5]

Unlike Musk's *Falcon 9*, the *New Shepard* that Bezos had launched did not include a commercial payload. The satellites the *Falcon* had sent into space would be used for years to come.

Once again, Elon Musk had succeeded. It was far from the first time that this determined man identified a problem, found solutions, and put them into action.

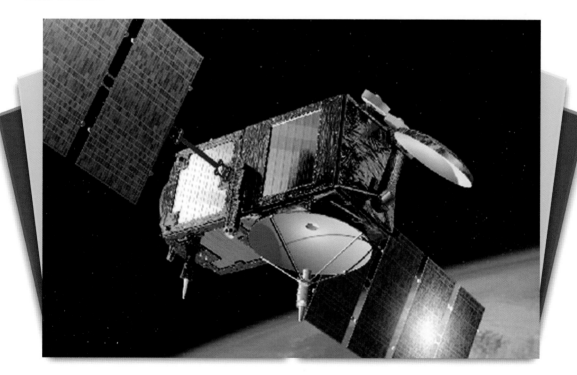

The Jason-3, a satellite that monitors the oceans, was deployed by Falcon 9 in January 2016. While Musk was not the first person to launch a privately funded rocket into space, he was the first to do so and deliver a payload.

Musk's life began in the southernmost country in Africa, called South Africa.

From the beginning, Musk kept his mother busy chasing after him.

Elon Reeve Musk was born on June 28, 1971, in Pretoria, South Africa. His British-Canadian mother, Maye, was a fashion model and dietitian. His South African father, Errol, was an electrical engineer. The family welcomed a second son, Kimbal, in September 1972, and a daughter, Tosca, in July 1974.

From the beginning, Elon was driven by curiosity. When he wanted to go to a friend's birthday party but was grounded, he decided to get there on his own. "It was clear across town, 10 or 12 miles away, further than I realized actually, but I just started walking," he recalled in an interview with *Fresh Dialogues*. "I think it took me about four hours … . My mother freaked out."[1] Most mothers would, since, at the time, Elon was only six years old!

When Elon was eight, his parents divorced. Tosca moved in with Maye, while Elon and Kimbal chose to live with their father. Life was not easy for the boys. Errol Musk was a difficult man. He lectured his sons for hours on end, not allowing them to speak. "It would certainly be accurate to say that I did not have a good childhood. It was not absent of good, but it was not a happy childhood," Musk recalls in a 2015 biography, *Elon Musk* by Ashlee Vance. "It was like misery," he added. "He [his father] is good at making life miserable—that's for sure. He can take any situation no matter how good it is and make it bad. He's not a happy man."[2]

One of the toughest challenges in Kimbal (center) and Elon's early life was dealing with Errol (left), a difficult and demanding father.

Kimbal agreed with his brother. "It was a very emotionally challenging upbringing, but it made us who we are today."[3]

School was also a rough place for young Elon—rough and dangerous.

The man who would one day astound the world with his ideas and successes was a shy, quiet child. According to his mother, Elon was "the youngest and smallest guy in his school. He didn't have friends." He loved books and computers and didn't care much about sports. "He was on computers as soon as they were available to us," Elon's sister Tosca told the *Business Insider*.[4] At the age of 10, he taught himself how to program and write code. At

The Commodore VIC 20 (keyboard shown) was the first computer on which Elon learned to program.

age 12, he created his own space game called *Blastar* and was selling it to other young gamers.

Elon often spent up to five hours a day reading everything from J.R.R. Tolkien's classic *Lord of the Rings* series to piles of comic books. One of his favorite books was the science-fiction novel *The Hitchhiker's Guide to the Galaxy*, by Douglas Adams. The book would inspire him throughout his life. "I was reading various books on trying to figure out the meaning of life, and what does it all mean," he recalls in an interview in *Fresh Dialogues*.[5]

The Hitchhiker's Guide to the Galaxy *cover*

The young daydreamer earned an unhappy reputation at school: as someone to bully.[6] One day, 12-year-old Elon and his brother Kimbal were sitting at the top of a flight of concrete stairs. Without warning, another student came up behind Elon and kicked him in the head. Elon tumbled down the stairs, where more kids were waiting. They pummeled him.

The beating put Elon in the hospital for two weeks. He was so mangled that his father did not recognize him. Although charges were filed, the police considered the incident a case of "schoolboy high jinks," so nothing was done.[7]

This attack changed the boy's life. "Kids gave Elon a very hard time," Kimbal told *Esquire*, "and it had a huge impact on his life, because there was no recourse."

Elon knew that he wanted out of his home in South Africa. He wanted to get away from the schools and the culture. As Kimbal said, "It's pretty rough in South Africa. It's a rough culture. Imagine rough—well, it's rougher than that." [8]

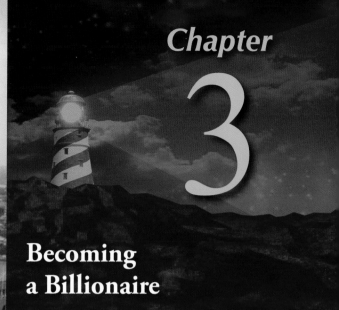

Jon M. Huntsman hall is the main building at the Wharton School, where Musk earned two degrees.

Becoming a Billionaire

Despite the bullies and the beatings, Elon graduated from high school at age 17. By then, he was fascinated with electronics and believed that North America was where he needed to go to explore the field. "[I]f you wanted to be close to the cutting edge, particularly in technology, you came to North America," he stated.[1]

His first move was to Canada in 1989, where his mother was a citizen. He attended Queen's University in Kingston, Ontario. Although he was working two jobs, Musk was struggling to make ends meet. The timing could not have been better when he was offered a full scholarship to the University of Pennsylvania's Wharton School of Business.

Finally, he had made it to the United States. At the Wharton School, he earned degrees in both physics and economics. What did he want to do with his new knowledge? "One was the Internet, one was clean energy, and one was space," he explained.[2]

After graduating, Musk moved to California, this time to attend Stanford University. He planned to earn his doctorate degree in applied physics. His mother, brother, and sister followed him to the United States.

Musk was at Stanford for only a few days when he made a new decision. The Internet was growing unbelievably fast, and, as Musk stated, "I could either watch it happen, or be part of it."[3]

As the Internet continued to grow, Musk used his programming skills to keep up—and to create businesses.

Two days after he started at Stanford, Musk dropped out. He and Kimbal had a new idea. It was called Zip2. The program allowed companies to place maps and directions on the Internet, as well as blogs—all commonplace now, but a new idea in the 1990s.

Their father loaned them the money to get started. Then the brothers took their idea to small newspapers and media companies.

"It was tough going," Elon said in an interview at Stanford University. "I didn't have any money. In fact, I had negative money." He had student debts to pay, and he could not afford a place to live. Instead, he lived in the back of the business office. "I just slept on the futon and showered at the YMCA," he admitted.[4]

Those rough days did not last forever, though. Musk spent four years developing Zip2—and ended up with a huge success. At the age of 28, he and Kimbal sold the software to Compaq Computers for $307 million.

The brothers were now technically millionaires. What would they do next? Kimbal went to culinary school and opened a line of restaurants. Elon stuck with technology. He founded an online payment company called X.com. This new service allowed people to email money to other people or companies with just a few clicks of the mouse. As the company expanded, it became known as PayPal.

By the end of the second year, PayPal had one million customers.[5] In 2003, Elon sold PayPal to Ebay—for $4.5 billion.

Both of Elon's businesses were successful, but they had more in common than that. They were both based on Internet software. They also were run by

PayPal headquarters are in San Jose, California, but the company is known throughout the world.

Justine Musk

"a small group of very talented people," as Elon stated in the interview at Stanford.[6] Both companies were dedicated to creating the best possible customer experience for people.

In January 2000, Elon Musk married novelist Justine (Jennifer) Wilson. The two had met at Queen's University in Ontario while they were teenagers. "I was a really lonely kid and he was a really lonely kid [growing up] and that's one of the things that attracted me to him," Justine told *Esquire*.[7] Musk knew right away that he wanted to date Justine, so he asked her out repeatedly. "The man does not take no for an answer," she recalled in his biography by Vance. "You can't blow him off. I do think of him as the Terminator. He locks his gaze on something and says, 'It shall be mine.'"[8]

The couple was married for eight years. During that time, they had six sons. Their first, a boy named Nevada, died at 10 weeks old. Later, in 2004, Justine gave birth to twins Griffin and Xavier, and then to triplets Damian, Saxon, and Kai in 2006. Two years later, Elon and Justine divorced.

Shortly after the divorce, Musk married a British actress named Talulah Riley. They were engaged 10 days after they met, and divorced two years after they were married. A year later, the two

Talulah Riley

remarried. Musk calls Riley "one of the most kindhearted and gentle people in the world."[9]

In 2002, Elon Musk officially became a U.S. citizen. He was far from finished starting companies, however. When asked why he did not just buy an island and retire, he told *Fresh Dialogues,* "The idea of lying on a beach as my main thing sounds horrible to me … . I would go bonkers … . I'd be super duper bored … . I like high intensity."[10]

Electric cars had long been a fascination for Musk, as well as space travel. Both were in his future.

While countless science-fiction fans have enjoyed reading about electric cars and space rockets, Musk did much more than just dream about them.

SpaceX is headquartered in Hawthorne, California. It features a huge hangar and launch pad for all of Musk's experiments and inventions.

Electric Cars and Space Travel

Anyone who had spent much time with Musk over the years knew he was interested in space travel. "I always thought we'd make much more progress in space . . . and it just didn't happen . . . it was really disappointing, so I was really quite bothered by it," he told *Fresh Dialogues*.[1] Musk often brought up the topic of space exploration, and even his father once said, "There's no doubt whatsoever; Elon is getting to Mars."[2]

In 2002, Musk took the millions he had earned from his prior business successes and put them into a new company called Space Exploration Technologies, or SpaceX. He believed that most Americans wanted to send rockets into space, but were reluctant to say so because of the billions of dollars it would cost.

"People came here from other places . . . people need to believe that it's possible so I thought it's a question of showing people there's a way," he stated in an interview with *Fresh Dialogues*. "There wasn't really a good reason for rockets to be so expensive. If one could make them reusable, like airplanes, the cost of rocketry (and space travel) would drop dramatically."[3]

The purpose of his new company was simple: to send a rocket to Mars. All Musk needed was the actual rocket. He tried to buy some from the Russians, but the military wanted far more money than Musk wanted to spend. He had another idea. He borrowed textbooks on rocketry and read them cover to cover.

"You know, whenever anybody asks Elon how he learned to build rockets, he says, 'I read books,'" Adeo Ressi, a friend of Musk's, told *Esquire.* "Well, it's true. He devoured those books."[4]

Musk was determined to build his own rocket, but other people were not so sure it was a good idea. A group of his friends and other space experts met with him to try to change his mind. "[We] all sat around a room and said, 'Elon, you cannot start a launch company. This is stupid,'" said Ressi. "Elon just said, 'I'm going to do it. Thanks.'"[5]

While Musk was working on creating his space company, he was also playing a large role in a company called Tesla Motors. The company focused on designing and building sporty electric cars, or cars run solely by battery.

The construction of Tesla vehicles depends largely on high-tech robotic arms like these.

Tesla headquarters, Palo Alto, California

Musk invested money in the company. By 2004, he was named Tesla's CEO (chief executive officer). "I tried really hard not to be the CEO of two startups at the same time," he admitted to *Fresh Dialogues*. "It's not appealing and shouldn't be appealing if anyone thinks that's a good idea. It's a terrible idea."[6]

As if he needed more hats to wear, Musk, along with his cousins, created a company in California in 2006 called SolarCity. "[T]he earth is almost entirely solar powered today," Musk stated in an interview. "The only reason we're not a frozen ice ball at 3 degrees Kelvin is because of the sun."[7] SolarCity provides solar-powered systems to thousands of office buildings and homes.

In 2012, co-founders Lyndon and Peter Rive celebrate the opening of SolarCity with their chairman, Musk.

Musk was right. Being in charge of all these huge and unusual companies was a lot for anyone to handle—even someone as talented and clever as Musk. After years of success, he began to face some failures. He would have to figure out how to deal with each one.

At SpaceX, Musk is involved in all stages of rocket production, including checking a future rocket's heat shield.

Primary

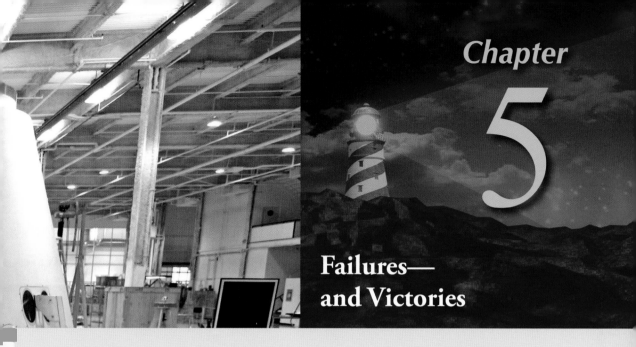

Musk's plans to put a rocket into space were progressing—slowly. By spring 2006, he actually had orders from companies to carry satellites into orbit. Even NASA was in on the plans. They donated millions to help Musk develop SpaceX. Now he only had one thing left to do: prove that his Falcon rockets could fly.

The first rocket was launched in 2006 from a small Pacific island. As it soared into the sky, everyone cheered. But 33 seconds into its flight, the engine caught fire. *Falcon 1* crashed to the ground, a burnt disaster.

A year later, the company tried again—and once more, the engine failed. In August 2008, a third Falcon was launched. This one was full of cargo from NASA and the U.S. Department of Defense. It also carried the ashes of James Doohan, the actor who had played Scotty on the original *Star Trek* TV series. The rocket crashed.

Musk's problems did not end there. Over at Tesla, there was big trouble brewing. Many people had prepaid for a Roadster, the company's first car. But Tesla was not producing the cars as planned. They did not have production money, and their federal loan had not yet arrived. Tesla was facing bankruptcy.

Musk laid off employees and closed some production centers. Then he did the only thing he could think of to save the company: he poured his personal money into it.

Kimbal Musk told *Esquire*, "Bankruptcy would have been easier than what he did. He threw everything he had into keeping Tesla alive."[1]

Meanwhile, on September 28, 2008, Musk launched his Falcon one more time. Adeo Ressi was there to see it. He told *Esquire*, "Everything hinged on that launch. . . . this was more than his fortune at stake—it was his credibility."[2]

The fourth time was the charm. The Falcon launched safely and disappeared into the sky overhead. Musk had not only produced his own rocket, but he had made it for a fraction of the cost of everyone else's rocket.

Finally, Musk's Falcon lifted off successfully.

Musk named his rocket after the **Millennium Falcon,** *the spacecraft piloted by Han Solo and Chewbacca in the original* **Star Wars** *movies.*

Although the launch was successful, Musk was out of money. He was considering shutting SpaceX down when he received a phone call from NASA. "NASA called and told us we won a $1.5 billion contract," Musk told *Space News.* "I couldn't even hold the phone. I just blurted out, 'I love you guys!'"[3]

SpaceX would keep working on the Falcon series until the successful launch and return on April 8, 2016. Since then, Musk has been using his rockets to send satellites into orbit and deliver supplies to the International Space Station.

Musk's next project for space travel was a familiar one: go to Mars—in less than 20 years. "I would like to die on Mars," the inventor has said. "Just not on impact." He added in an interview with *Telegraph* that going to Mars "will be the greatest adventure ever. I personally am motivated more by the second, that it would be a fantastic and exciting adventure."[4]

In 2014, Musk showed off his manned **Dragon** *capsule, designed to carry as many as seven astronauts into space.*

Tesla vehicles are assembled by robots, which are run by technicians.

Tesla also made a turnaround. The Roadster began winning awards. It was followed by the popular Model S, an electric sedan. *Time* magazine named the Model S one of the 25 Best Inventions of 2012, and *Motor Trend, Automobile Magazine*, and others voted it Car of the Year in 2013. By 2015, Tesla was worth over $30 billion.[5]

The Tesla Roadster 2.5

Musk has not slowed down, at work or at home. When he did not like the school choices open to his five sons, he fixed the problem like he did at work: he created his own. In the fall of 2015, Ad Astra School had 20 students, including Musk's sons and the children of SpaceX employees. "I didn't see the regular schools doing the things I thought should be done," he said on *Business Insider*.[6] Ad Astra, which does not have separate grades, focuses on teaching problem-solving skills. Its name means "To the Stars."

Meanwhile, Musk came up with yet another project: the Hyperloop. This futuristic type of travel would allow people to ride from one large city to the next in plastic vacuum tubes. The tubes would be solar-powered and move at speeds of up to 700 miles per hour. He presented the idea to investors in 2013, and by 2016 Hyperloop Technologies was using Musk's original concept to build the system on a campus in downtown Los Angeles.

By age 44, Musk was worth more than $8 billion. The world was hopeful that he would continue to come up with new ideas and then chase after them with his trademark courage, curiosity, and conviction.

On April 8, 2016, **Falcon 9** *successfully landed on a SpaceX drone ship in the ocean. Reusable rockets were now a reality.*

1971 Elon Musk is born in South Africa on June 28.

1983 He invents the videogame *Blastar* and sells it to friends.

1988 He graduates from Pretoria Boys High School.

1991 Musk graduates from University of Pennsylvania with bachelor's degrees in physics and business. He then enrolls in Stanford University, but drops out after two days and moves to Silicon Valley.

1995 He and his brother, Kimbal, release Zip2.

1999 The brothers sell Zip2 to Compaq. Elon creates X.com, the future PayPal.

2000 Elon marries Justine Wilson.

2001 Musk establishes the Musk Foundation to provide grants for renewable energy, space and medical research, and science and engineering education.

2002 Musk becomes an American citizen and founds SpaceX.

2003 He sells PayPal to Ebay for $4.5 billion.

2004 He invests in Tesla Motors. Twins Griffin and Xavier are born.

2006 Musk helps to create SolarCity. Triplets Damian, Saxon, and Kai are born.

2008 Musk becomes chief executive officer (CEO) of Tesla Motors. He and Justine Wilson divorce.

2010 Musk marries Talulah Riley. They divorce two years later.

2013 Musk suggests the idea of the Hyperloop travel system. He remarries Talulah Riley.

2015 On December 21, Musk successfully launches a reusable rocket into orbit and brings it back safely.

2016 Musk's *Falcon 9* successfully launches *Jason-3*, a satellite that will collect data on Earth's oceans. The Falcon then lands safely on a platform in the ocean.

Chapter 1

1. Julie Johnsson and Dana Hull, "Musk Greets SpaceX Reusable Rocket With 'Welcome Back, Baby,'" *Bloomberg*, December 21, 2015, Updated December 22, 2015.

2. Ben Rooney, "Amazon Founder Jeff Bezos' Space Company Launches First Rocket into Space," *CNN Money*, April 30, 2015.

3. Johnsson and Hull.

4. Editorial Board, "Elon Musk's SpaceX Aces It with *Falcon 9* Touch Down," *The Sacramento Bee*, December 25, 2015.

5. " 'Welcome Back, Baby': Elon Musk Celebrates SpaceX Rocket Launch—and Landing," *The Guardian*, December 22, 2015.

Chapter 2

1. Alison Van Diggelen, "Elon Musk: His Remarkable Story in His Own Words," *Fresh Dialogues*, January 29, 2013.

2. Ben Rooney, "What Makes Elon Musk Tick?" *CNN Money*, May 14, 2015.

3. Marvin Meint Jies, "Elon Musk: How a Bullied Boy Became a Man Who Can Change the World," *The Times*, May 31, 2015.

4. Nicholas Carlson, "Elon Musk Was Bullied and Lonely as a Kid—Then He Found Computers and Business," *Business Insider*, December 23, 2013.

5. Van Diggelen.

6. Carlson.

7. Alec Hogg, "Errol Musk: 'Elon Was Beaten So Badly, I Couldn't Recognize Him," *BizNews.com*, July 22, 2015.

8. Tom Junod, "Elon Musk: Triumph of His Will," *Esquire*, November 14, 2012.

Chapter 3

1. Evan Carmichael, "The Wired Entrepreneur: The Early Years of Elon Musk," undated.

2. Ibid.

3. Ibid.

4. "History of Zip2," *Stanford University's Entrepreneurship Corner*, October 8, 2003.

5. "Success Through Viral Marketing: PayPal," *Stanford University's Entrepreneurship Corner*, October 8, 2003.

6. Ibid.

7. Tom Junod, "Elon Musk: Triumph of His Will," *Esquire*, November 14, 2012.

8. Justine Musk, " 'I Was a Start Wife': Inside America's Messiest Divorce," *Marie Claire*, undated.

9. Elon Musk, "Elon Musk: Correcting the Record about My Divorce," *Business Insider*, July 8, 2010.

10. Alison Van Diggelen, "Elon Musk: His Remarkable Story in His Own Words," *Fresh Dialogues*, January 29, 2013.

Chapter 4

1. Alison Van Diggelen, "Elon Musk: His Remarkable Story in His Own Words," *Fresh Dialogues*, January 29, 2013.

2. Kabous Le Roux, "We Interview Errol Musk, Father of the Most Innovative Entrepreneur of Our Age." *702*, May 6, 2015.

3. Van Diggelen.

4. Tom Junod, "Elon Musk: Triumph of His Will," *Esquire*, November 14, 2012.

5. Ibid.

6. Van Diggelen.

7. Ibid.

Chapter 5

1. Tom Junod, "Elon Musk: Triumph of His Will," *Esquire*, November 14, 2012.

2. Ibid.

3. Brian Berger, "Why SpaceX's Elon Musk Says 2008 Was His 'Worst Year' Ever," *Space News*, April 3, 2014.

4. Andrew Smith, "Meet Tech Billionaire and Real Life Iron Man Elon Musk," *The Telegraph*, January 4, 2014.

5. Ben Rooney, "What Makes Elon Musk Tick?" *CNN Money*, May 14, 2015.

6. Maya Kosoff, "Elon Musk Didn't Like His Kids' School, So He Made His Own Small, Secretive School without Grade Levels," *Business Insider*, May 22, 2105.

PHOTO CREDITS: Cover—John Voo; P. I—InInnovation; pp. 4, 6, 8. 9. 12, 16, 24—Public Domain; p. II—Benjamin Ragheb; p. 14—bixblock; p. I5—Sagar Savla; p. I8—Nasa.gov; pp. 20, 22, 26—Steve Jurvetson; p. 2I—Citi Informi, Tumbehhaur; p. 25—Tim Bailey; p. 27—Maurizio Pesce. All other photos—cc-by-sa-2.0. Every measure has been taken to find all copyright holders of material used in this book. In the event any mistakes or omissions have happened within, attempts to correct them will be made in future editions of the book.

Books

Doeden, Matt. *SpaceX and Tesla Motors Engineer Elon Musk* (STEM Trailblazer Bios), Lerner Classroom, 2015.

Elon Musk: *Quotes from the Greatest Entrepreneurs.* Av2 by Weigl, 2015.

Jordan, Hal. *101 Facts about Elon Musk: 101 Facts about Elon Musk You Probably Never Knew.* Amazon Digital Services, 2015.

Pauline T. *Elon Musk: Biography of the Mastermind Behind PayPal, SpaceX and Tesla Motors.* Amazon Digital Services, 2012.

Skuzynski, Gloria. *This Is Rocket Science: True Stories of the Risk-taking Scientists Who Figure Out Ways to Explore beyond Earth.* National Geographic Children's Books, 2010.

Works Consulted

Berger, Brian. "Why SpaceX's Elon Musk Says 2008 Was His 'Worst Year' Ever." *Space News,* April 3, 2014. http://www.space.com/25355-elon-musk-60-minutes-interview.html

Carlson, Nicholas. "Elon Musk Was Bullied and Lonely as a Kid—Then He Found Computers and Business." *Business Insider,* December 23, 2013. http://www.businessinsider.com/elon-musk-was-lonely-2013-12

Carmichael, Evan. "The Wired Entrepreneur: The Early Years of Elon Musk." Undated. http://www.evancarmichael.com/library/elon-musk/The-Wired-Entrepreneur-The-Early-Years-of-Elon-Musk.html

Editorial Board. "Elon Musk's SpaceX Aces It with *Falcon 9* Touch Down." *The Sacramento Bee,* December 25, 2015. http://www.sacbee.com/opinion/editorials/article51364395.html

"History of Zip2." *Stanford University's Entrepreneurship Corner,* October 8, 2003. http://ecorner.stanford.edu/authorMaterialInfo.html?mid=397

Hogg, Alec. "Errol Musk: 'Elon Was Beaten So Badly, I Couldn't Recognize Him.'" *BizNews.com,* July 22, 2015. http://www.biznews.com/undictated/2015/07/22/errol-musk-elon-was-beaten-so-badly-i-couldnt-recognise-him/

Jies, Marvin Meint. "Elon Musk: How a Bullied Boy Became a Man Who Can Change the World." *The Times,* May 31, 2015. http://www.timeslive.co.za/sundaytimes/opinion/2015/05/31/Elon-Musk-How-a-bullied-boy-became-a-man-who-can-change-the-world

Johnsson, Julie, and Dana Hull. "Musk Greets SpaceX Reusable Rocket With 'Welcome Back, Baby'" *Bloomberg,* December 21, 2015, Updated December 22, 2015. http://www.bloomberg.com/news/articles/2015-12-22/musk-s-spacex-returns-to-space-in-first-launch-since-june-blast

Junod, Tom. "Elon Musk: Triumph of His Will." *Esquire,* November 14, 2012. http://www.esquire.com/news-politics/a16681/elon-musk-interview-1212/

Kosoff, Maya. "Elon Musk Didn't Like his Kids' School, So He Made His Own Small, Secretive School without Grade Levels." *Business Insider,* May 22, 2105. http://www.businessinsider.com/elon-musk-creates-a-grade-school-2015-5

Le Roux, Kabous. "We Interview Errol Musk, Father of the Most Innovative Entrepreneur of Our Age." *702,* May 6, 2015. http://www.702.co.za/articles/2761/we-interview-errol-musk-father-of-the-most-revolutionary-entrepreneur-of-our-age

Musk, Elon. "Elon Musk: Correcting the Record about My Divorce." *Business Insider,* July 8, 2010. http://www.businessinsider.com/correcting-the-record-about-my-divorce-2010-7

Musk, Justine. " 'I Was a Start Wife': Inside America's Messiest Divorce." *Marie Claire,* undated. http://www.marieclaire.com/sex-love/advice/a5380/millionaire-starter-wife/

Rooney, Ben. "Amazon Founder Jeff Bezos' Space Company Launches First Rocket into Space." *CNN Money,* April 30, 2015. http://money.cnn.com/2015/04/30/news/jeff-bezos-rocket-launch/

Rooney, Ben. "What Makes Elon Musk Tick?" *CNN Money,* May 14, 2015. http://money.cnn.com/2015/05/14/news/elon-musk-biography/

Smith, Andrew. "Meet Tech Billionaire and Real Life Iron Man Elon Musk." *The Telegraph,* January 4, 2014. http://www.telegraph.co.uk/technology/news/10544247/Meet-tech-billionaire-and-real-life-Iron-Man-Elon-Musk.html

FURTHER READING

Van Diggelen, Alison. "Elon Musk: His Remarkable Story in His Own Words." *Fresh Dialogues*, January 29, 2013, http://www.freshdialogues.com/2013/01/29/elon-musk-his-remarkable-story-in-his-own-words-video/

"'Welcome Back, Baby': Elon Musk Celebrates SpaceX Rocket Launch—and Landing," *The Guardian*, December 22, 2015. http://www.theguardian.com/science/2015/dec/22/welcome-back-baby-elon-musk-celebrates-spacex-rocket-launch-and-landing

On the Internet

Elon Enthusiast (Observing the Life and Times of Elon Musk)
http://elonenthusiast.com/

Launch: *Jason-3* Webcast
http://www.spacex.com/webcast/

SolarCity: "About Solar City"
http://www.solarcity.com/company

SpaceX
http://www.spacex.com

Tesla Motors: "About Tesla"
https://www.teslamotors.com/about

GLOSSARY

bankruptcy (BANK-rupt-see)—The protected legal status of a person or company that is unable to pay its debts.

cargo (KAR-go)—Goods carried as freight by sea, road, air, or space.

citizen (SIH-tih-zen)—A person who has the right to live in a country and the right to the legal and social benefits of that country.

credibility (kreh-dih-BIL-ih-tee)—The quality of inspiring belief.

deploy (dee-PLOY)—To send out or place in a position for a particular purpose.

dietitian (dy-eh-TIH-shin)—Someone who is trained in how the body uses food.

doctorate (DOK-tur-it)—The highest degree given by a university.

intensity (in-TEN-sih-tee)—The degree or quality of power, strength, or concentration.

Kelvin (KEL-vin)—The metric measurement of temperature based on absolute zero.

orbit (OR-bit)—The path of a planet, satellite, or moon around another body in space.

payload (PAY-load)—The amount of equipment and people in a spacecraft.

reputation (reh-pyoo-TAY-shun)—The opinion or views that people have of another person or thing.

satellite (SAT-uh-lyt)—A device that orbits a planet to send communication signals or other information.